Pebble® Plus

E**X**treme Animals

# The Most Dangerous Animals

by Connie Colwell Miller

**Consulting Editor:** Gail Saunders-Smith, PhD

**Consultant:** Tanya Dewey, PhD
University of Michigan Museum of Zoology

CAPSTONE PRESS
a capstone imprint

Pebble Plus is published by Capstone Press,
151 Good Counsel Drive, P.O. Box 669, Mankato, Minnesota 56002.
www.capstonepub.com

 Books published by Capstone Press are manufactured with paper
containing at least 10 percent post-consumer waste.

*Library of Congress Cataloging-in-Publication Data*
Miller, Connie Colwell, 1976–
 The most dangerous animals / by Connie Colwell Miller.
  p. cm. — (Pebble plus. Extreme animals)
 Includes bibliographical references and index.
 Summary: "Simple text and photographs present the world's most dangerous animals"—Provided by publisher.
 ISBN 978-1-4296-5312-1 (library binding)
 ISBN 978-1-4296-6210-9 (paperback)
 1. Dangerous animals—Juvenile literature. I. Title.
QL100.M55 2011
591.6'5—dc22                                                                                2010028755

**Editorial Credits**
Katy Kudela, editor; Heidi Thompson, designer; Marcie Spence, media researcher; Laura Manthe, production specialist

**Photo Credits**
Alamy: Biju, 17, Redmond Durrell, cover; Ardea: Valerie Taylor, 21; Minden Pictures: Toshiji Fukuda, 15; Photo
Researchers, Inc.: Scott Camazine, 5; Seapics: Gary Bell, 11; Shutterstock: Andre Bonn, 7, Chris Alleaume, 19,
efendy, 9, kkaplin, 13, Vladimir Korostyshevskiy, 1

# Note to Parents and Teachers

The Extreme Animals series supports national science standards related to life science.
This book describes and illustrates dangerous animals. The images support early readers in
understanding the text. The repetition of words and phrases helps early readers learn new
words. This book also introduces early readers to subject-specific vocabulary words, which are
defined in the Glossary section. Early readers may need assistance to read some words and to
use the Table of Contents, Glossary, Read More, Internet Sites, and Index sections of the book.

Printed in the United States of America in North Mankato, Minnesota.
092010     005933CGS11

# Table of Contents

# Dangerous

They chomp! They sting!

They shred with their claws!

These animals aren't just scary.

Their danger is EXTREME.

One Africanized honeybee is a

bother. A swarm is dangerous.

These bees can kill when

they attack in groups.

4

More than 200 kinds of
poison dart frogs live in
Central and South America.
These frogs are small, but
their bright skin is poisonous.

A scorpion jabs with its stinger.

One sting freezes a bug, spider,

or small lizard in its tracks.

The scorpion munches its prey.

# More Dangerous

A box jellyfish's tentacles grow up to 10 feet (3 meters). One sting from these tentacles can stop a large fish's heart within minutes.

Beware!

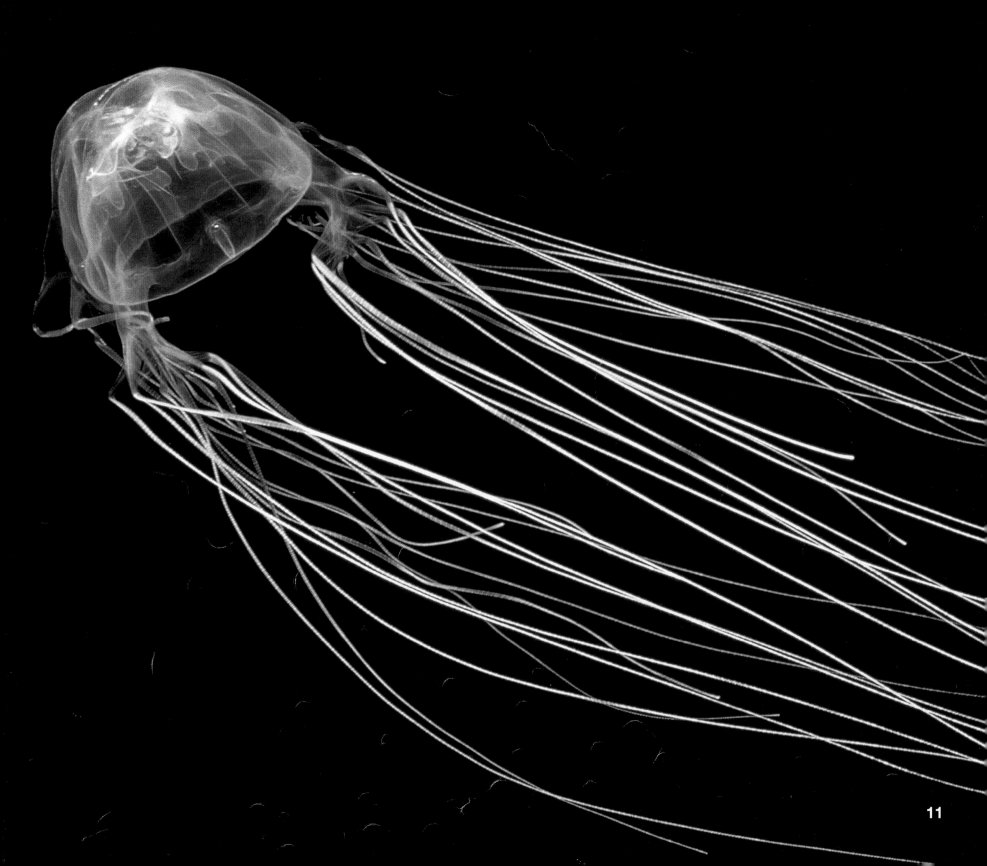

The Komodo dragon

has a venomous bite.

Its mouth is full of germs too.

One bite will kill an animal

in just a few days.

A hunting Siberian tiger

will not give up.

It follows and waits. Pounce!

The tiger's 3-inch (8-centimeter)

claws tear its prey to pieces.

# Most Dangerous

Watch out! A king cobra with

its hood raised is dangerous.

Its bite has enough venom

to kill an elephant.

Hippos only eat grass,

but other animals stay away.

They don't want to upset a hippo.

Angry hippos chase and trample

when they feel threatened.

In the ocean, the great white shark is king. This giant shark has more than 3,000 teeth. It chomps seals, dolphins, and small whales too.

# Glossary

germ—a very small living thing that can cause disease

hood—part of a cobra's neck

poison—a substance that can kill or harm someone if it is swallowed, inhaled, or touched

prey—an animal that is hunted by another animal for food

stinger—a sharp, pointed part of an insect or animal that can be used to sting

swarm—a group of insects that gather or move in large numbers

tentacle—a long flexible structure usually around the head or mouth of an animal

trample—to damage or crush something by walking heavily all over it

venom—poison produced by some snakes, spiders, and other animals

# Read More

**Miller, Connie Colwell.** *The Creepiest Animals.* Extreme Animals. Mankato, Minn.: Capstone Press, 2011.

**Stout, Frankie.** *Nature's Deadliest Animals.* Extreme Animals. New York: PowerKids Press, 2008.

# Internet Sites

FactHound offers a safe, fun way to find Internet sites related to this book. All of the sites on FactHound have been researched by our staff.

Here's all you do:

Visit *www.facthound.com*

Type in this code: 9781429653121

Check out projects, games and lots more at **www.capstonekids.com**

23

# Index

Word Count: 226

Grade: 1

Early-Intervention Level: 19